FAITH AND FREEDOM BASIC READERS

These Are Our Friends
REVISED EDITION

Sister M. Marguerite, S.N.D., M.A.

Sister M. Bernarda, C.PP.S., PH.D.

GINN AND COMPANY
Boston • New York • Chicago • Atlanta
Dallas • Palo Alto • Toronto

ACKNOWLEDGMENTS

Grateful acknowledgment is made to the following authors and publishers for permission to use copyrighted material:

Sally Aldrich Adams for "Little Bus Gets a New Job," adapted from "The Small Bus Gets a New Job," reprinted by special permission from *Jack and Jill,* copyright 1952, by The Curtis Publishing Company; Leone Adelson for "The Blow-away Hat," adapted from *The Blow-away Hat,* published by David McKay Company; Educational Publishing Corporation for "The Best Place in the World," adapted from "The Nicest Place in the World," by Katherine L. Edgerly, reprinted from *Grade Teacher Magazine* by special permission; Holiday House for "A Birthday Box for Pete," adapted from *The Birthday Story,* by Ruth Jaeger Buntain; Helen Pettigrew for "Where Are a Cow's Ears?" adapted from "Where Are Flossie's Ears?" reprinted by special permission from *Jack and Jill,* copyright 1957, by The Curtis Publishing Company; Val Teal for "The Funny Little Farm," adapted from "A Very Stylish Farm," copyright 1945, by *Child Life Magazine,* reprinted by permission of the author; The Viking Press for "A Prayer," from *In and Out, by Tom* Robinson, copyright 1943, by Tom Robinson, reprinted by permission of The Viking Press, Inc.; Whitman Publishing Company for "The Old Street Car," based on "The Noisy Little Streetcar," by Betty Ren Wright, from *Big, Big Story Book,* copyright 1955, by Whitman Publishing Company and reprinted by permission of Whitman Publishing Company; Catherine Woolley for "A New Home for Gabriel," adapted from "A Garage for Gabriel," from *American Junior Red Cross News,* copyright 1947, by American National Red Cross.

Illustrations by Albert Jousset, Ralph Shepherd, Margot Locke, and Dorothy Tainter.

FAITH AND FREEDOM

NIHIL OBSTAT:

Rev. Gerard Sloyan, s.t.l., ph.d., censor deputatus

IMPRIMATUR:

† Patrick A. O'Boyle, d.d., archbishop of Washington

Washington, December 15, 1960

COMMISSION ON AMERICAN CITIZENSHIP
THE CATHOLIC UNIVERSITY OF AMERICA

Rt. Rev. Msgr. William J. McDonald, *President of the Commission*

Rt. Rev. Msgr. Joseph A. Gorham, *Director*

Katherine Rankin, *Editorial Consultant*

Sister Mary Lenore, o.p, *Curriculum Consultant*

PUBLISHED FOR THE CATHOLIC UNIVERSITY OF AMERICA PRESS
WASHINGTON, D.C.

Stories in This Book

■ Friends at Home

■ Friends at School

■ The Children's Story Book Friends

■ Friends Who Help Us

■ Story Time with Grandmother

Friends at Home

The Little House

Tom was David's friend.
He went to school with David.

One day Tom said,
"Come to my house, David.
Come and see my house.
It is not like your house."

Mother said David could go
to Tom's house.

"You will like my new house,"
Tom told David.
"We can ride in our house.
I can go to bed and ride.
I can play in the house and ride."

"That must be a funny house,"
said David.

"See, here it is," said Tom.

"This is where I live.
This is our new house."

"Is that a house?" David said.
"It looks like a big bus."

"Come in," said Tom.
"Come in and see our house."

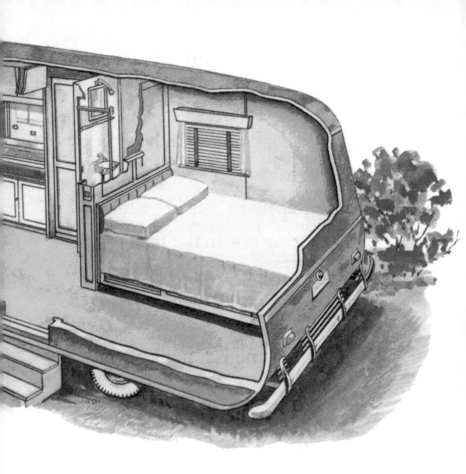

"It must be fun to live
in this house," said David.

"It is fun," laughed Tom.
"We work and play in this house.
And we can take a ride in it, too."

David told his family all about Tom's new house.

Daddy said, "Tom's family is happy in that new house.
We are happy in our little house.
A house can not make us happy.
But we can make a house a happy home to live in."

"And our home is a happy one," said Mother.

The Cars That Ran Away

One day Timmy wanted to play
with his toy cars.

He went to the toy box
to get them.

He saw the little red car.

He saw the little blue car.

But the yellow car
was not in the toy box.

Timmy went to Mother.

"Oh, Mother," he said.

"I want to play with my cars.
But my little yellow car
has run away."

"A toy car could not run away,"
said Mother.

"Did you look in the toy box?"

"The blue car is in the box,"
said Timmy.

"The red car is in the toy box.
But where can my yellow car be?"

"Play with the red car
and the blue car," said Mother.
"Maybe you will find the other car."

Timmy looked in the toy box.
What a surprise he had!
The blue car was not in the box.
It was not in the room.

"Where can it be?" he said.
"It was here with the red car."

"Oh, Mother," said Timmy.
"What can I do?
My blue car has run away, too."

"Did you put it in the toy box?"
Mother said.
"Maybe you put it
in the other room."

Mother and Timmy looked
for the blue car.
They looked in Ann's room.
They looked in Timmy's room.
But they did not find it.

Mother and Timmy went
into Daddy's room.

They laughed and laughed.

They saw the blue car.

They saw the little yellow car.

And they saw Zip, too.

"Oh, Mother," said Timmy.
"See where Zip put the cars.
He wanted to surprise Daddy.
What a funny surprise!"

Ann's New Book

Ann ran into the house.
"Look, Mother," she said.
"See this new book!
It is a book about Jesus.
I can read some of it."

Ann began to read for Mother.
But she could not read all the book.

Daddy came home.

He saw Ann's new book.

"We can all read this book," he said.

"I will read some of it.

Mother can read some of it.

You and David can read, too."

The family sat down.

Daddy began to read about Jesus and the children.

Jesus was tired.

He wanted to rest.

He wanted to pray, too.

He wanted to pray to God,
His Father.

Jesus sat down to rest
and to pray.

But He did not rest.

He did not pray.

Some little children saw Jesus.

"We want to go to Jesus,"
they said.

The mothers came
with the children.

They, too, wanted to see Jesus.

A friend of Jesus saw the children.

He wanted Jesus to rest.

So he went to the mothers.

"Take your children home,"
he said.

"Jesus is tired.

He wants to rest."

Jesus looked at the man.
"Do not tell the children
to go away," He said.
"I love little children.
They are My friends.
I want them to come to Me."

So the children ran to Jesus.
He loved all of them.
He made them happy.

Timmy and Pam

Timmy and Pam played all day.
They played house.
They played store.
They had fun with Zip
and the kittens.
They played with other children, too.

One day Pam said to Timmy,
"Come and see what I have.
It is a surprise.
My daddy gave it to me."

"Oh, a white bunny!" said Timmy.
"It looks like a white ball.
A funny little white ball!"

"See the bunny hop," said Pam.
"Hop, little bunny, hop, hop."

The white bunny began to hop.
The children began to hop, too.

Zip saw the white bunny.
He saw the bunny go hop, hop, hop.
He saw the children hop.
Zip began to hop, too.
But he could not do it.
He looked as funny as could be.

The Bunny's Lunch

One day Timmy went
to Pam's house for lunch.

The children had a good lunch.

They wanted White Bunny to have
a good lunch, too.

So they got some cookies.

Little White Bunny ate and ate.
He ate a dish of cookies.
It was not a good lunch
for a bunny.

After lunch, White Bunny
did not want to play.
    The children called and called.
    Come, little bunny," said Pam.
    "Hop, hop, hop."

    The bunny did not come.
    He did not hop.
    He sat and looked at the children.

"Maybe our bunny is tired,"
said Timmy.

So the children got a box.

They made a bed for the bunny.

They told White Bunny to sleep.

After that, the children
went to Timmy's house.

Little White Bunny did not sleep.
He was not happy.
He wanted something green to eat.

So he got out of the box.
He began to hop, hop, hop.
Away he went to find
something green to eat.

After that the bunny ran away.
Timmy and Pam looked and looked.
They called and called.
They could not find White Bunny.

The bunny went to live
with his animal friends.
He wanted to eat what they eat.
He did not want cookies
for his lunch.

Birthday Surprises

David and Ann did not know what to do.

Mother's birthday was here.
And they had no surprise for her.

"What can we do?" Ann said.
"What can we get Mother for her birthday?"

"Mother wants a new white hat," David said.
"Maybe Daddy will get one for her."

"Maybe we could get her a book,"
Ann said.

"Mother likes to read.
She likes candy, too.
We could get her a box of candy."

"We can not do that," David said.
"We have no money.
You have no money.
And I have no money."

That night, Ann told David
something.

"I know what we can do
for Mother's birthday," she said.

"It is a funny birthday surprise.
Maybe Mother will like it."

David laughed.

"That will be a good surprise,"
he said.

Mother's birthday came.
David and Ann jumped out of bed.
They began to get breakfast.
When Mother came down, they said,
"Happy birthday, Mother!"

They gave Timmy his breakfast.
They gave the baby her breakfast.
After breakfast, they made
the beds.

"We will help you all day, Mother,"
they said.

When night came,
the children went to bed.
They went before Mother told them.
They said, "Happy birthday
and good night, Mother."

"This was a happy birthday,"
Mother said.
"Thank you for all the surprises."

"We had fun, too,"
said David and Ann.
"Birthday surprises are fun."

The Blow-away Hat

Daddy gave Mother a new hat
for her birthday.

It was a green and white hat.
Mother liked her new hat.

One day Daddy said,
"This is a good day for a walk.
We will all go for a walk."

So Mother put on her new hat.
Daddy put on his hat.
And the family went for a walk.

The wind began to blow.
Away went Mother's new hat!
"Oh, my new hat!" said Mother.

"We will run after it,"
said David and Ann.
And away they went.
"I can get it," said Daddy.

Away he went, down the street.
They all began to run
after Mother's blow-away hat.

"I have it," called Daddy.

But before he could get it,
a big bus came by.

The wind began to blow and blow.
And away went Mother's hat!

"Where did it go?" said Ann.

"The wind took it up the street,"
said Daddy.

Daddy and the children began
to run up the street.

The children saw a big hole.
It was in the street.
"What is that?" David said.

"That is a man-hole," said Daddy.
"A man can go down into it.
He can work down in the hole."

That day a man was at work
in the man-hole.

The man came up.
He looked at the children.
He did not know about the hat.

Daddy and the children
laughed and laughed.
They told the man about the wind
and the hat.
The man in the hole laughed, too.
And David took the blow-away hat
to Mother.

The Show Man and His Dog

One day all the children
saw something funny.

They called David and Ann
to come out and see it.

"Here comes the show man,"
said one of the boys.

"His little dog is with him."

All the children ran to see
the show man.

The show man began to play.
Toot! Toot! Toot!
The little dog put on
a funny show for the children.
The children laughed and laughed.
What fun they all had!

The show man called his dog.
The dog jumped up on the man.
He took a green box
and went to David.

David said, "Is that box for me?"

Oh, I know what that is for,"
said Tom.

"The dog wants us to put money
into the box.

He wants money for his show.

We must go home and get
some money."

All the children began to run.
Some ran up the street.
Some ran down the street.
They all wanted to get money
to put in the little green box.

The children came back.
Some of them had money,
and some did not.

Mother told David and Ann
that she had no money to give them.
   They did not want to go back
with the other children.

   Mother said, "I will give you
a big red apple.
   Maybe the show man will like that."

David and Ann ran back
to the street.
And Timmy was with them.
They gave the apple
to the show man.

"Thank you," said the show man.
"I like apples."

He began to eat the apple
and to walk down the street.
And his little dog ran after him.

Friends at School

The Surprise Box

Sister Jean had a big white box.
Sometimes she put a surprise in it.
Sometimes the children put
surprises in the box.

One day David and Ann
had a surprise to put into the box.
"You may put it in the box,"
said Sister.
"The boys and girls will like it."

The other children saw the box
They wanted to look in.

No, no," Sister Jean said.
"David and Ann will show us
the surprise."

"Is it a little animal?" said Tom.
"Can it grow?" said Mary.
"Maybe it is a flower," Bill said.

David said, "It can grow.
Some day it may be a flower."

Ann took the surprise
out of the box.

"Here are some flower seeds,"
she said.

"We can plant them.
Maybe they will grow."

"That will be fun," said all
the children.

"I will help you plant the seeds,"
said Sister Jean.

The children put the seeds
in a big brown box.
They gave them water.
They put them in the sun.

"Flower plants must have sun,"
Sister told the children.
"We must see that our plants
have sun and water."

One day the children
saw a pretty yellow flower.

"The flower is God's surprise,"
Sister Jean told the children.
"God made the flower grow
from a little seed."

That day the children went
to church.
They gave the flower to Jesus.
"You made it grow," they said.
"We want You to have it."

Seeds to Eat

"I ate some seeds today," said Tom.

"Seeds?" said Ann.
"Did you eat flower seeds?"

"No," laughed Tom.
"They were not flower seeds."
"Were they apple seeds?"
said Mary.

"Apple seeds are brown," Tom said.
"The seeds I ate were green."

"What kind of seeds could they be?"
David said.

Sister Jean laughed.
"We all eat seeds sometimes,"
she said.
"Some kinds of seeds are good to eat.
Some are not good for us to eat.
I will show you some of the seeds
we can eat."

Sister Jean began to show
the children all kinds of seeds.
Some were yellow.
Some were brown.
Some were green.

"I can show the kind of seeds
Tom ate today," David said.
"See, here they are."

"The brown seeds look like nuts,"
Ann said.

"Nuts are seeds too," said Sister
"They grow on trees."

"Do seeds grow in us
when we eat them?" said Ann.

"No, Ann," said Sister Jean.
"Seeds must be put into the ground.
They grow into plants.
All plants have seeds.
We eat some of the seeds.
Birds and animals eat seeds, too.
And some seeds are put back
into the ground to make new plants."

A Birthday Box for Pete

Betty lived on Water Street.

Sometimes she went home for lunch.

One day Betty saw something
on the ground.

It was a little box.

A little box with yellow paper on it.

On the box it said,
"A Happy Birthday to Pete."

"Oh, my, who is Pete?" said Betty.
"He has lost his birthday surprise."

She looked up and down the street.
Pam lived in the yellow house.
Mary lived in the brown house.
A new family lived in the
white house.
Who could Pete be?

Betty ran into her house.

She took the pretty box with her.

"Do you know who Pete is, Mother?"
she said.

"No," said Mother, "I do not.

After lunch you can go
to the new house up the street.

Maybe Pete lives in that house."

Betty ate her lunch.

After that, she ran up the street.

No one in the new house
was named Pete.

So Betty took the birthday box
to school.

As she went up the street,
a big brown dog ran to her.

He jumped up and said,
"Bow-wow-wow."

"Down, Pete!" someone called.
A big boy came to help Betty.
She told him about the box
with Pete's name on it.

"Oh, that is for my dog,"
said the boy.
"Today is his birthday.
Mrs. Ball gave the box to me.
I must have lost it."

The boy took the paper
from the box.
Pete jumped up and down
when he saw what was in it.
"Bow-wow," he said.
And he ate his birthday surprise.

The New Boy

One morning David and Ann were
in school before the other children.

"Good morning," said Sister Jean.

"May we help you, Sister?"
said Ann.

"We will water the plants.

We will get out the work papers."

Soon a man came into the room.
He had a little boy with him.
The man had to help the boy walk.

David and Ann went to the boy.
"We are happy to see you,"
they said.
"We are David and Ann.
What is your name?"

"My name is Jim," said the new boy.

Soon the other children came
into the room.

They saw the new boy who
could not walk.

They all told Jim that they
were happy to have him with them.

Tom gave Jim some books to read.
Bill told Jim about the surprise box.
Then school began.

Soon it was time to go out to play.

David went to Sister Jean.

"May I play here in the room
with Jim?" he said.

He will have no one to play with."

"It is good of you to want
to help Jim," said Sister Jean.

"God loves all children.

He wants us to love them, too."

Some of the other boys saw David.

"We want to play with Jim, too," they said.

"I have my wagon here," said Tom.
"We can take Jim for a ride."
The boys took Jim out in the wagon.
They all had a good time.
They made Jim happy.
They made God happy, too.

Tom Finds Out

Tom looked in his pocket.
"Where is my money?" he said.
"I had it this morning.
I put it in this pocket."

Tom went to Sister Jean.
"Someone took my lunch money,"
he said.
"I put it in this pocket.
Now it is not here."

"Look in your other pocket,"
said Sister.

"Maybe you lost the money
when you went out to play."

"Oh, no, Sister," said Tom.
"Someone in this room took it.
And I know who it is.
David had money for candy today.
I saw him in the store this morning."

Sister Jean called David.
She asked him about Tom's money.

"I did not take the money,"
David said.
"My daddy gave me a dime.
He gave Ann a dime, too."

"You took my money," said Tom.
"You know you did."

David did not know what to do.
He called Ann and said something.

Then Ann looked at Tom.
"I will give you my dime," she said.
"You can give it back to me
when you find your money."

Ann gave her dime to Tom.
She had wanted to get some
pretty paper with it.

All that day, Tom did not look
at David.

He did not play with him.

He did not want the other boys
to play ball with David.

After school, Tom did not walk home
with David and Ann.

When Tom got home,
he saw something.

The money was in his bed room!

Tom went to his mother.
"Oh, Mother," he said.
"I told Sister Jean
that David took my money.
I told all the children, too."

"That was not kind of you,"
Mother said.
"You must do something.
You must make up for what
you said about David."

Tom ran back to school
He told Sister Jean about the money.
Then he went to David's house.
I want to take back what I said,"
Tom told David.
"And here is Ann's dime."

In the morning, Tom told
all the children something.
"David did not take my money,"
he said.
"It was at home."
After that, Tom and David
were good friends.

The Squirrel That Went
to School

One day David was going to school.
He saw something on the ground.
He called some of the other boys
to come and see it.

"What is it?" asked Bill.
It is a baby squirrel," David said.
"See, it can not walk.
It can not run."

Bill had some nuts in his pocket.
He gave them to the little squirrel.
But the squirrel did not eat them.

The boys took the squirrel to school.
They asked Sister Jean if they
could take care of it.

Sister Jean was happy to have
the children take care of the squirrel.
"God made the animals," she said.
"He made them for us.
He wants us to take care of them."

The children got a box.

They made a nest for the squirrel.

Then they put the squirrel
into the box.

They put a dish of water in the box.

They put some nuts in the box too.

"This is fun," said one of the girls.

"It is fun to take care
of this baby squirrel."

Soon the little squirrel began to eat.
He liked the nuts the children
gave him.

He began to grow too.

One morning, he gave the boys
and girls a surprise.
He got out of his nest.
He jumped up on some books.

"Look at our squirrel," said Ann.
"See him go!"

Up and down, in and out
ran the squirrel.

"We must take the squirrel
back to his mother now," said Sister.

"He can not live in a room like this
all the time."

So the children said good-by
to the little squirrel.

That day some of the boys took him
back to the tree.

When Mother Squirrel saw her baby,
she came down to get him.

Then she ran up the tree,
and the baby squirrel ran after her.

The squirrels were happy.

The children were happy, too.

The Party Dress

All the girls at school were asked to Betty's birthday party.

Ann was asked to the party, too.
She wanted a new dress for that day.

"Oh, Mother," Ann said.
"May I have a pretty new dress for the party?"

"No, Ann," said Mother.
"You have one good dress.
We can not get a new one."

"But, Mother," said Ann.

"All the other girls will have
pretty new dresses.
I want a new dress, too.
Will you get one for me?"

"No, Ann," Mother said.
"Your blue dress is pretty.
We have no money for a new dress."

Ann was sad.

She did not go out to play
with David and the other children.

She did not play with her toys.

When Daddy came home,
he saw Ann in the house.

She was crying.

"Did someone do something
to you today, Ann?" he asked.

"You look so sad."

Ann looked at Daddy.
"I want a new dress
for Betty's party," she said.
"Mother will not get it for me.
All the other girls will have
new dresses.
I want a pretty new dress, too."

Daddy sat down with Ann.

He said, "A new dress will not make you happy, Ann.

Pretty things do not make us happy.

When we are good, we are happy.

When we do what God wants, we are happy.

But money and pretty dresses do not make us happy.

Run out and play now.

When the day for the party comes, you will be happy."

The Birthday Party

The day for the party came.
Some little girls had pretty dresses.
Some had dresses that were not
so pretty.

One little girl had on an old dress.
It was not pretty at all.
But the little girl looked happy.
She laughed and played.
She had fun with the other children.

One of Ann's little friends had on
a new white dress.

It was pretty.

No other girl had one like it.

When the children began to play,
the little girl would not play.

"I must take care of my new dress,"
she said.

Betty's mother gave the children some candy.

The little girl in the new white dress would not eat hers.

"I do not want to get candy on this new dress," she said.

The little girl in the new dress did not have a good time.

Her dress was pretty.

But she was not happy.

That night Ann told
Mother and Daddy about the party.
She told about the little girl
in the new white dress.

"She did not have fun," Ann said.
"All she did was take care
of her pretty dress.
She could not play with us.
She could not eat candy.
She just sat and looked pretty."

The Children's Story Book Friends

The Little Red Hen

One morning Mrs. Goose saw
Little Red Hen going by.
"Where are you going,
Little Red Hen?" she asked.

"I want to find something good
to eat," said Little Red Hen.
And away she went.
Soon Little Red Hen saw
something yellow on the ground.

"Wheat!" she said.
"This wheat will make something
good to eat."

Little Red Hen looked
at the other animals.
"Who will help me
plant this wheat?" she asked.

"Not I," said the duck.
"Not I," said the goose.
"Not I," said the pig.

"Then I will," said Little Red Hen.
"I will plant this wheat."
And she did.

Soon the wheat began to grow.
It was time to cut it down.

Little Red Hen went
to her animal friends.
"Who will help me cut this wheat?"
she asked them.

"Not I," said the duck.
"Not I," said the goose.
"Not I," said the pig.

"Then I will cut it,"
said Little Red Hen.
"I will cut this wheat."
And she did.

"Now I will make some bread,"
said Little Red Hen.
"Who will help me
make the bread?"

"Not I," said the duck.
"Not I," said the goose.
"Not I," said the pig.

"Then I will," said Little Red Hen.
"I will make the bread."
And she did.

Then Little Red Hen said,
"Who will help me eat this bread?"

"I will," said the duck.
"I will," said the goose.
"So will I," said the pig.
And they all ran to get some bread.

But Little Red Hen said
"Cluck, cluck, cluck.
You will not eat this bread.
My little chicks and I will do that."
And they did!

The Pancake Man

A little old man and woman
lived in a little old house.

One morning the little old woman
made a pancake.

She called the little old man
to see it.

"That pancake looks good,"
said the little old man.

"I am going to eat it."

Just then the pancake jumped out
of the pan.

Away it went.

It ran out of the house.

It ran down the street.

The little old woman
ran after the pancake.

The little old man ran, too.

"Stop, stop, Pancake!" they called.

But the pancake did not stop.

It ran on and on and on.

The little old man and woman
could not catch the pancake.
So they went back to the house.

Soon a big dog saw the pancake.
"Stop, Pancake, stop!" said the dog.

The pancake did not stop.
It ran on and began to sing

"I am the Pancake Man.
Try to catch me if you can.
I ran away from a little old woman
and a little old man.
I can run away from you, too, I can."

The dog ran and ran.
But he could not catch the pancake.

Soon a goat saw the pancake.
"Stop, Pancake!" called the goat.
"I want to eat you up."

The pancake laughed
and began to sing,
"I am the Pancake Man.
Try to catch me if you can.
I ran away from a little old woman
and a little old man.
I can run away from you, too, I can."

And the goat could not catch him.

Then the pancake saw a fox.
"How pretty you sing," said the fox.
"Will you sing for me?"

So the Pancake Man sat down
by the fox and began to sing

"I am the Pancake Man.
Try to catch me if you can . . ."

"You will not run away from me,"
said the fox.
"I am going to eat you up."
And that is just what the fox did!

The Boy and the Goats

A little boy had some goats.

All day they ran and played and ate out on the green hill.

At night, the boy took them home.

One night, the boy went to get the goats.

When the goats saw him, they ran back up the hill.

The boy could not get them to come down.

So he sat down and began to cry.

Just then a rabbit came by.

"Why do you cry, little boy?"
asked the rabbit.

"I can not get my goats down
from the hill," the boy said.

"I can get them," said the rabbit.
The rabbit called and called.
But the goats would not
come down.

So the rabbit sat down
with the boy and began to cry.

Soon a fox came by.

"Why do you cry?" asked the fox.

"I cry because the boy is crying,"
said the rabbit.

"He is crying because his goats
will not come down the hill."

"I can get them," said the fox.

The fox called and called.

But the goats would not come down.

So the fox sat down with the rabbit
and the boy.

The fox, too, began to cry.

Then a little bee came by.
"Why do you cry?" asked the bee.

The fox said, "I cry because
the rabbit is crying.
The rabbit is crying because
the boy is crying.
He is crying because his goats
will not come down the hill."

"Oh, I can get them," said the bee.
"How can a little bee do that?"
laughed the boy and the animals.

The little bee went up the hill.
"Z-z-z-z-z-z," he said.

The goats jumped up
and ran down the hill.
They ran home as fast
as they could go.

And that is how the little bee
got the goats down the hill.

Little Bus Gets a New Job

Little Green Bus had a big job to do.

All day he ran up and down the streets.

He took people to work.

He took mothers to the stores.

He took boys and girls to school.

So, when night time came, the little bus was tired.

One night, Little Green Bus
went home to rest.

He had a surprise.

But it was not a happy surprise.

He saw a big new yellow bus.

"Who are you?" asked
the little bus.

"And why are you here?"

"I am here because I came
to take your job," said the yellow bus.

"You are too little.

The people want a big bus."

This made Little Green Bus sad.

In the morning, a man came.
He got into the yellow bus.
He took it out and rode away.

"Oh, my," said Little Green Bus.
"No one cares for me now.
No one wants to ride in me."

So, day after day, the sad little bus
sat at home.

Then one day, a man and a woman
came to look at the little bus.

"It is a good bus," the bus man
told them.

"Just too little, that is all."

"We will try it," said
the man and woman.

"We will see how it runs."

Now the little green bus
began to be happy.

"Br-r-r-r-r-r," he said
when the man and woman got in.

The next morning, a man came
to work on the little bus.

He made it a pretty yellow.

Soon it looked as pretty
as the big new bus.

One day the man came back.

He took the little bus out.

Away they went.

Then they came to some children
with school bags and books.

"Here comes our new school bus,"
the children said.

They got into the bus.

The little bus was happy.

"Now I have a good job," he said.

A New Home for Gabriel

Gabriel was a little car
that had no home.

Day after day, he sat out
in the sun and the wind.

People looked at him.
But no one wanted him.
Gabriel was too old.

"I am not a new car," Gabriel said.
"I am not pretty.
But I do want a home."

One day a little old woman came to look at cars.

"Have you a little car for me?" she asked the man.

"I have this little car," he told her. "It is not the best one we have. But it is good for an old car."

"I will take a ride in it," said the old woman. "Maybe it is just what I want."

Now Gabriel was happy.
He wanted the little old woman
to like him.

"I will do my best," he said.
"I will show this little old woman
how fast I can go."
And away Gabriel went,
as fast as he could go.

"Oh, my!" said the little old woman.
"This car is too fast for me.
I do not want it."

The next day a big boy
came to get a car.

He saw the little old car.

"I want to see how this car runs,"
he said.

So he got into the car
and rode away.

"This time I will do my best,"
said Gabriel.

"I will not go fast.

I will go slow because I want
the boy to like me.

I want him to take me home."

"What a slow old car this is,"
said the boy.

"I do not want this car.

It is too slow for me."

Then a man came to look at cars.
He wanted to try the little old car.

"This time I will not go slow,"
said Gabriel.
"I will not go fast."

The man got into the car.
"Bang-bang, bang-bang,"
went Gabriel.

"Oh, oh, oh," said the man.
"I do not want this car.
This is not the car for me."

By this time, Gabriel was sad.
He was as sad as he could be.
But soon a man and a little boy
came to look at cars.
They rode in the little car.

Gabriel did not go bang-bang.
He did not go too fast.
He did not go too slow.

"This is just the kind of car
we want," the man said.

So away went Gabriel with the man and the little boy.

Soon they came to a pretty yellow house.

The little boy's mother came out to look at the little car.

Then the man put the car away for the night.

Now Gabriel had a home.

He was a happy little car.

The Best Place in the World

Mother Rabbit began to read
a story to Bunny Rabbit.

It was about the best place
in the world.

But Mother Rabbit went to sleep.

So Bunny Rabbit did not find out
where that place was.

"I will try to find it," he said.
Away he went, hop, hop, hop.

Soon Billy Goat saw Bunny Rabbit
"Stop, Bunny Rabbit," he said.
"Where are you going so fast?"

"I can not stop now," said Bunny.
"I am going to find the best place
in the world."

"That place must be far away,"
Billy Goat said.

"I do not care how far it is,"
said Bunny Rabbit.
"I am going to find it."

"Then I will go with you,"
said Billy Goat.

So away they went.
They did not go far before they met
Mrs. Squirrel.

"Stop, Friends!" called Mrs. Squirrel.
"Why must you run so fast?"

"We are going to find the best place
in the world," said Bunny Rabbit.

"Do you know where it is?"
asked Mrs. Squirrel.

"No," said Billy Goat.
"But we are going to find it."

"I want to see the best place
in the world," said Mrs. Squirrel.
"I will go with you."

Next the animals met
Mrs. Red Bird.

"Stop, stop!" she called
when she saw them.

"Where are you going so fast?"

"We want to find the best place
in the world," they told her.

"Do you know how to get there?"

"Yes," said Mrs. Red Bird.
"It is not far away.
You must go up this hill.
Walk to the old apple tree.
And there you will find
the best place in the world."

The animals said thank you
to Mrs. Red Bird.
And away they went.
They ran up the hill.
Then they looked for the old
apple tree.

"There it is," said Mrs. Squirrel.

And do you know what they saw?

It was Bunny Rabbit's home.

Bunny Rabbit looked at Billy Goat and laughed.

Billy Goat looked at Mrs. Squirrel and laughed.

"Maybe this was in the story," said Bunny Rabbit.

"But, you see, my mother went to sleep.

After all, home is the best place in the world for all of us."

Friends Who Help Us

Surprises Here and There

Timmy sat up in bed.
He looked here and there.
This did not look like his room.
Just then Grandmother Green
came into the room.

"Now I know where I am,"
Timmy said.
"This is your house, Grandmother."
"Yes, it is," said Grandmother.
"Did you forget that you came
to see me?"

Timmy ate a good breakfast.

Then he and Grandmother began
to walk to the store.

Soon they came to Hill Street.

Grandmother said, "Can you guess
what is on this street, Timmy?

It is the home of our best Friend."

"Pam is a good friend,"
Timmy said.

"But she lives far away."

Then Grandmother and Timmy
came to a big church.

"Do you know Who lives in there?"
Grandmother asked.

"Yes," said Timmy.
"That is God's house."

Timmy and Grandmother went
into the church.

They prayed to Jesus,
the Son of God.

Then they came out
and went on up the street.

Soon they came to the next street.
"There is another surprise
on this street," said Grandmother.
"Can you guess what it is, Timmy?"

"Maybe it is a place where the bus
stops," said Timmy.
"Then we can ride to the store."

But there was no bus stop
on that street.

There were all kinds of stores.
One was a toy store.
One was a flower store.
There was a book store too.
But Grandmother took Timmy
into another kind of store.

In that store, Timmy saw
all kinds of good things to eat.
He saw big cakes and little cakes.
He saw cookies, buns, and bread.

Grandmother got some cookies.
Then she and Timmy came
out of the store.

"Where are we going now?"
Timmy asked.

"On the next street there is
another surprise," said Grandmother.

"Oh, Grandmother," said Timmy
"I am tired.
I do not want another surprise.
I just want to go home."

Then Timmy saw his house.
David and Ann ran to him.
Little Mary was with them.
They were happy to see Timmy.
And Timmy was happy to be home.

"Oh, Grandmother," said Timmy.
"This is the best surprise of all.
There is no place like home."

The Fire House

One morning David and Ann
ran to school.

When they got there,
they saw a big blue bus.

"Hop in," said the bus man.
"This bus will take you
to the fire house."

Down the street went the big
blue bus.

Soon it came to the fire house.

Sister Jean and the children got out.

"Here comes a fireman," said Tom.
"Maybe he will show us
the fire house."

The children said good morning
to the fireman.
"We are happy to be here,"
they told him.

"Come with me," said the fireman.
"I will show you the fire house."

Sister Jean and the children
went with the fireman.

The children saw some big trucks.
"What big red trucks!" they said.

"We ride on the trucks when we go
to a fire," said the man.
"All the cars on the street
stop when they see us.
People know that we are going
to a fire.
They know that we must get there
as fast as we can."

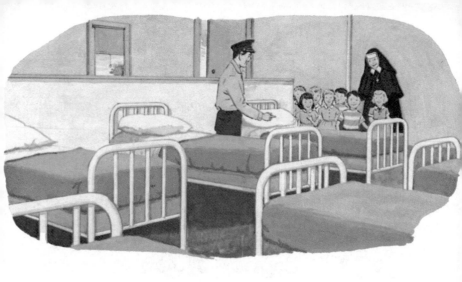

Then the children saw some beds.
"Beds in a fire house!" said Bill.
"Why do you have beds here?"

The fireman said, "We have them
because some men must live here.
They must eat and sleep here."
"What if the men are in bed
when there is a fire?" asked David.

The fireman laughed.
"They have to get up as fast
as they can," he said.

"Look at that man!
Where is he going?" asked Tom.

"Oh, he is just going down,"
the fireman said.
"We all go down like that.
We have no time to walk
when there is a fire.
We must get down as fast
as we can."

Soon the children heard something.
Clang! Clang! Clang!

"There! That is a fire,"
said the fireman.

He took the children away
from the place where the trucks were.

The men jumped up on the trucks.
Clang! Clang! Clang!
Away they rode as fast as they
could go.

What Will You Be?

"When I grow up I am going to be a cowboy," said Tom.

"I am going to be a fireman," said David.

"I want to be a Sister like Sister Jean," said Betty.

"Maybe I will take care of sick people," Ann said.

Mother heard the children.

"Maybe some of you will be God's helpers," she said.

"How can we do that?" asked Tom.

"I know," said Betty.
"Mothers and fathers are God's helpers.

They tell us about God.

They tell us about Mother Mary and Saint Joseph.

They help us to pray."

"Yes," said David's mother.
"Good mothers and fathers help God.

But God has other kinds of helpers, too."

"Who are they?" asked Ann.

"I will tell you about
one of them," Mother said.
"This helper gives Jesus to us.
He takes Jesus to the sick.
He helps people to know about God."

"That is Father Brown," said Betty.

"Yes," said Mother.
"Father Brown is a priest.
And every priest is one
of God's best helpers."

"Here comes Father Brown now," said David.

"Oh, Father Brown," said Tom.
"David's mother told us that you are one of God's best helpers."

"Yes," said Father Brown.
"Every priest is God's helper.
But God wants more priests to do His work."

"That is what I will be when I grow up," said David. "I will be a priest like you."

"So will I," said Ann.

Everyone laughed. "Girls can not be priests," said Tom.

"No, Ann," said Father Brown. "Girls can not be priests. But girls, too, can help God. They can be Sisters."

"That is what I want to be," said Betty.

"You can help God now,"
Father Brown told the children.
"You can pray for more priests
and Sisters to do His work."

Every day after that David and Ann
said this to God:
"Oh, Jesus, make many more boys
want to be priests.

Make many more girls want to be
Sisters.

Give us more priests and Sisters
to do Your work."

A Friend in Blue

David and Ann were going to school.
They met some friends.
Tom had his wagon with him.
In the wagon, there was
a little brown and white dog.

"What a pretty little dog!"
said Ann.
"Are you going to take him
to school?"

"Yes," said Tom.
"I want Sister Jean to see my dog."

All the children began to walk
to school.

Before they got to the next street,
the little dog jumped out of the wagon.

Away he ran up the street.

The children ran after him.

Then the little dog ran into
the street.

Cars were going up and down
the street.

There were big trucks too.

"Oh, my dog!" said Tom.
"How can we catch him?"

The little dog ran here and there.
He ran up and down.
He did not know where to go.

"Toot, toot!" went the cars.
"Toot, toot, toot!" went the trucks.

A man in blue was out in the street.
He heard the cars and trucks toot.
He heard the little dog cry.
So he made all the cars stop.
He made the trucks stop, too.
Then he got the little dog
and gave it back to the children.

"Thank you," said the children.
"It was kind of you to help us."

The man in blue said, "That is
my job.
I am here to help people like you.
Run on to school now."

The happy children went on.
This time they did not put
the little dog in the wagon.
One boy took the dog.
Another boy took the wagon.
And soon they were in school.

To the Farm

One morning a friend of Daddy's
took David and Ann to see his farm.
They rode there in a big truck.

The children did not see many houses.
"Where are the houses?"
Ann asked.

"The farms out here are big,"
said the farmer.
"But there is a house
on every farm."

"Here we are," said the farmer.
"This is my farm.
Hop out and we will go to see
the animals."

They did not have to go far.
A big brown cow came to them
and said, "Moo-moo-moo!"
The two children laughed
and said moo-moo to the cow.

Two yellow kittens came up
to David and Ann.
"Mew, mew," they said.

Then the farmer took them
to the hen house.

They heard the hens go
cluck, cluck, cluck.

There were many hens and chicks
in the hen house.

"I would like to take care
of the baby chicks," Ann said.

"They would make good pets."

"Oh, come here, Ann," David called.
"See what is in this nest."

A big white hen had just jumped
from the nest.
"Cluck, cluck," she said.

You can guess what the
two children saw.
Two white eggs in the nest!

"I guess we will have eggs
for lunch today," said the farmer.
"Two eggs for two children."

Next the farmer took the children to see the ducks.

"Now I will show you another kind of egg," he said.

He gave David a big egg.

"What kind of egg is that?" asked David.

"It is as big as two hen eggs.

"This is a duck egg," said the farmer.

The hungry children ate
a good lunch.

They had home-made bread.

They had milk from the cows.

They had eggs from the hens.

They had apples and other good things
to eat.

After lunch, the children went to see
the pigs and the goats.

"Do you know what goats eat?"
the farmer asked.

"Apples," said David.

The farmer laughed and said,
"Goats are hungry animals.

They try to eat all kinds of things.
They like paper and old cans."

"Oh, my," said Ann.
"I would not want to be a goat."

"I must get you home
before dinner," the farmer said.

So the two children said good-by
to the animals.

The animals said good-by, too.
"Moo, moo, moo!"
"Quack, quack, quack!"
"Cluck, cluck, cluck!"

And one began to crow,
"Cock-a-doodle-do!"

When they got home, they said
thank you to the farmer.

"Come now," Mother said.
"You are tired and hungry.
You must have some dinner
and then go to bed.
We will all thank God
for the good time you had today."

Our Best Helper

One day the children named
all the helpers they had met.

"There is another Helper,"
Daddy said.
"You did not name Him.
But He is our best Friend
and Helper."

"Is it someone in this house?"
David asked.
"You and Mother help us
all the time."

"Yes, we help you," said Mother.
"But not like our best Helper."

Daddy said, "That helper is God's Son.

God gave Jesus to us.

Jesus helps us.

He asks His Father to give us what we pray for."

"I know another helper," Ann said.

"It is Mother Mary.

We ask her to help us.

We ask her to pray for us."

"Saint Joseph helps us, too," Mother said.

"He lives with God.

He can tell God what we want."

"God loves Mother Mary
and Saint Joseph.

That is why we pray to them.

We can tell them to ask God
for what we want."

"There are other helpers
who live with God," said Daddy.

"Who are they?" David asked.

"We named Jesus, Mary,
and Saint Joseph."

"The angels are helpers," said Daddy.

"The angels help people.
You have an angel to help you.
Mother's angel helps her.
My angel helps me.
Timmy, too, has an angel helper."

"What about Baby Mary?" asked Ann.

"Is she too little to have an angel?"

"God gave the baby an angel when He made her," Daddy said.

"Our angels are with us all the time."

"Some day our angel will take us back to God.

Then we will see God.

We will live with Him.

We will live with Jesus.

We will see Mother Mary and Saint Joseph.

We will see all the angels.

And with them, we will be as happy as can be."

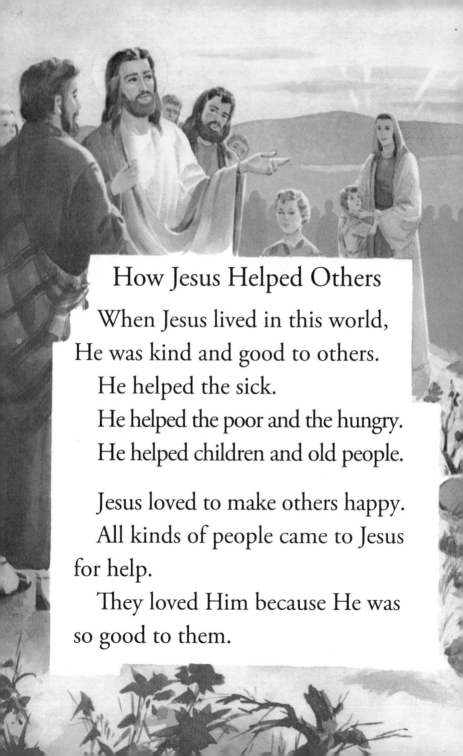

How Jesus Helped Others

When Jesus lived in this world,
He was kind and good to others.
He helped the sick.
He helped the poor and the hungry.
He helped children and old people.

Jesus loved to make others happy.
All kinds of people came to Jesus
for help.
They loved Him because He was
so good to them.

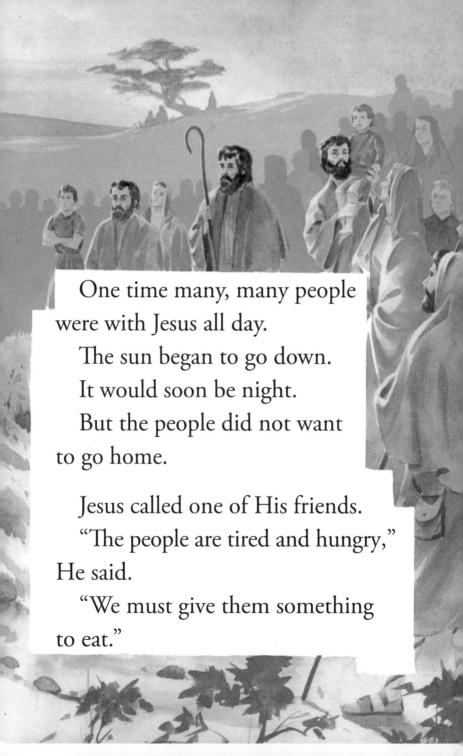

One time many, many people were with Jesus all day.

The sun began to go down.

It would soon be night.

But the people did not want to go home.

Jesus called one of His friends.

"The people are tired and hungry," He said.

"We must give them something to eat."

Jesus' friend looked at Him.
"We can not find food
for so many people," he said.
"Tell the people to go home.
Then they can get something
to eat."

"No," Jesus said.
"I do not want the people
to be tired and hungry.
We must give them something
to eat before they go home.
Have we no food here?"

"There is a boy here," said the man.
"He has a little food with him.
But what can we do with that?
There are many, many people here."

Jesus said, "Tell the boy to come here."

Soon the little boy with the food came to Jesus.
Jesus took the food and prayed.

Then Jesus called His friends.
He gave the food to them.
"Take this food," He said.
"Give some to all the people."

The people sat down on the ground.
They all had something to eat.
And then there was some food
to give away to the poor.

When the people saw this,
they were surprised.
"Jesus must have come from God,"
they said.
"God is with us."

Story Time with Grandmother

The Funny Little Farm

A little old woman lived on a farm.
She had two little boys, a cow,
a pig, a dog, and some hens.

One day the little old woman said,
"All we do in this place is work.
I am tired of work.
I would like to dress up and
look pretty."

So this is what the little
old woman did.

She put on her best dress.
She got some new boots for the boys.
She got a new hat for her cow.
She cut two holes in the hat.
Then she put it on the cow.

After that she made the
other animals look pretty.
  "Come with me now," she said.
"We will not work.
We will just look pretty."

So they all sat and sat and sat.

The cow could not eat because
she could not see with the hat on.

The boys could not play because
they had on new boots.

The hens could not run to
the hen house.

Soon the little old woman got tired.
She was hungry, too.

"Oh, I am as hungry as can be," said the litle old woman.

"I would like to have some dinner. I would like to milk the cow. I would like to get the eggs. I would like to make some bread. But I can not work because I have on my best dress."

She looked at the two boys. They looked tired and hungry, too. They did not like the new boots. She looked at the animals. They did not look happy.

No one could do what he wanted to do.

So this is what the little old woman did.

She took off her best dress
and got out the old one.
She told the boys
to take off the new boots.
She took off the cow's pretty hat.

The little old woman went
back to work.
She began to get dinner.
The little boys ran to milk the cow.
The pig began to look for food.
The hens went to the hen house.
And everyone was happy.

The Old Street Car

Mrs. Toot lived in a little place called Green Hill.

Not many people lived there.

One street car ran in and out of Green Hill every day.

"Bang, bang, bang," went the little old car.

One day Mrs. Toot met Mrs. Bee.

"We must have a new bus,"
said Mrs. Toot, "A bus that will not
go bang, bang, bang all the time."

"This is a good street car,"
said Mrs. Bee.

"How would we know the time
if it did not go bang, bang?"

"Oh, go on," said Mrs. Toot.
"We must have a new bus.
And that is that!"

One day a new blue bus
took the place of the old street car.

The new bus did not go bang, bang.
So no one heard it.

No one was out on time to
catch the new bus.

Men were not on time for work.

Children were not on time
for school.

"Well," said Mrs. Toot.

"I guess there is something
to be said for that old street car."

"I told you so," said Mrs. Bee.

The next morning, the people
of Green Hill heard something.

It was not the new blue bus.

It was the little old street car.

"Bang, bang," it said as it came
down the street.

All the people were happy to see it.

And after that, everyone was
on time.

Where Are a Cow's Ears?

Ted lived on a farm.

Every day he rode to school
in a big yellow bus.

Some of the children who rode
on the bus did not live on farms.

One day a little girl said to Ted,
"Where are a cow's ears? We must know
before we read our new books."

All the children looked at Ted.

"They are in the same place as every other animal's," said Ted.

"But a cow has horns, too," said the little girl.
"Are the ears in back of her horns?"

Ted began to get red.
"Maybe they are," he said.
"Yes, I guess they are in back of her horns."

Before Ted got off the bus,
he said something to the bus man.

No one heard but the bus man.

"Do you know where a cow's ears
are?" Ted asked the man.

"Well, if you do not know,
how can I?" the bus man said.

"After all, you live on a farm.
I do not. But I will tell you
in the morning."

When Ted got home, he said, "Mother, where are the cow's ears?"

Mother laughed and said, "Why do you want to know? Has she lost them?"

"No," Ted said, "she has not. I just want to know where they are. Are they in back of her horns?"

"Well, now," said Mother. "Maybe they are. Maybe they are not. Go and ask Grandmother."

Ted ran out to Grandmother. "Do you know where the cow's ears are?" he asked.

"I know that I do not have them," laughed Grandmother.

"I did not know she had lost them."

Then Ted asked what he wanted to know about the cow's ears.

"Are they in back of her horns?"

"Well, now," Grandmother said. "They are in the same place they were when you got that cow."

"I will go and look at our cow,"
Ted said. "Then I will know where
her ears are."

So off he ran to the place where
the cow was.

There he saw Mother, the bus man,
and Grandmother.

They all looked at Ted and laughed.

"I guess we all came here
for the same thing," said Mother.
    They all looked and looked
at the cow's ears and horns.
    "Now we all know,"
said the bus man.

    And they did.
    But do you?

Just One Day

Sometimes Peter was a good boy.
Sometimes he was not so good.
There was one thing that Peter
did not like to do.

And that was to do as he was told.

When Mother told him to do
something, he said, "I do not want to."
He said the same thing to Daddy.

One day Peter said, "I would like to do what I want for just one day."

"Well, you may do that," said his mother.
"But on that same day, I will do just what I want, too."

The next morning, Peter got up when he wanted.
He was going to eat what he wanted for breakfast.
But there was no breakfast.

Peter ran to Mother's room.

Mother was in bed.

"Oh, Mother," he called.

"I want some breakfast."

"I know that," said Mother.

"But this is my day to do
what I want.

I want to rest now

I do not want to get breakfast."

The little boy began to look
for something to eat.

There was no bread.

There were no eggs.

There was no milk in the house.

"Oh, Mother, I am so hungry,"
Peter said.

"I can not find a thing to eat."

"Well, you see," said Mother.
"You did not want to go
to the store for me.

That is why we have no milk
and bread and eggs.

This is my day to do what I want.
I do not want to go to the store."

Peter went out to play ball.

When he came in for lunch,
there was no lunch.

The house did not look
as it did on other days.

Peter's bed was not made.

His cowboy boots were on the bed.

His hat was there, too.

But this was Mother's day
to do what she wanted.

And now she wanted to look at TV.

She did not want to do house work.

Before dinner, Peter went
to Mother.

He began to cry.

"I am not happy," he said.

"I do not want another day
like this one.

I will do what you want, Mother."

"Yes," said Mother
 "We must help one another.
We can not do just what we want."

After that day, Peter did
what others wanted.

He helped Mother and Daddy
when they asked him.

And they all were happy.

Grandmother's Best Story

Jesus is the Son of God.
God made us.
He made this world for us.
He gives us everything we have.

One time Jesus lived in this world.
He came here to show people
how to live.
He did not have all the things
we have.

Jesus was poor because He wanted
us to know that He loves the poor.

Many times Jesus was tired
and hungry.

Jesus is the Son of God.
But He did His work
just as other men have to do.

He helped the poor and the sick.
He told the people about God.

Jesus wants us to live as He lived.
He wants us to be kind to others.
He wants us to help
the poor and the sick.

He wants us to do as we are told.
He wants us to pray
and to ask Him for help.

Jesus wants us to love Him.

Jesus, the Son of God, died for us.
He died to show us that He loves us.
He died so that we could live
with Him some day.

Now we can not see Jesus
as we see other people.
He is with His Father.
But Jesus is in the Church too.

Jesus loves us.
And he wants us to love Him. too.

The children heard something.
It was Daddy.
He had just come home from work.

"It must be time for us
to help Mother," Ann said.

So Grandmother and the children
went to help Mother.
After dinner, Timmy told Daddy
the story of how Jesus died.
He told how Jesus loved us
and died for us.

A Prayer

Tell me what to say, God,
Help me say it;
Tell me what to pray, God,
Help me pray it.

Tell me what to see, God,
Help me see it;
Tell me what to be, God,
Help me be it.

Tell me what to do, God,
Help me do it,
Anything for You, God,
If I only knew it.

Tom Robinson

To the Teacher

These Are Our Friends, Revised Edition, is the first reader of the FAITH AND FREEDOM Basic Readers. It extends the basic vocabulary by 157 words, 109 of which (starred in the list below) the pupil can recognize independently by means of the various word-recognition techniques developed in the manuals of the preceding texts and continued in the manual accompanying the first reader. The 167 words introduced in the preceding books of the series are repeated in this book.

Concepts of Christian social living in the family, church, school, and community are developed throughout the first-reader level. The child is led to realize his dependence upon God for all things and to recognize the manifestations of Divine Providence in his daily life through the love and kindness of others with whom he works, worships, and plays. Continued emphasis is given to the virtue of love.

Word List

Unit I			Unit II
	21 so*	34 breakfast	
7 friends	22 . . .	when	47 . . .
8 Tom*	————	35 before*	48 some-
9 new*	23 Pam*	————	times*
10 live	24 white	36 blow*	may*
11 . . .	ball*	walk	49 grow*
12 family	25 hop*	37 wind*	flower
————	26 got*	street*	50 seeds*
13 blue*	27 after	38 by*	plant*
14 has*	called*	took*	51 water
15 room	28 sleep*	39 hole	sun*
16 put	29 green*	40 . . .	52 from*
17 . . .	eat*	————	————
————	30 . . .	41 show*	53 today*
18 book*	————	him*	were
read	31 birthday	42 toot*	54 kind*
19 sat*	her	43 . . .	55 nuts*
children	32 money*	44 back	trees*
20 tired	33 night	45 give*	56 ground
rest*		46 . . .	————

191

DEFGHIJKL 06987654

PRINTED IN THE UNITED STATES OF AMERICA